I0527937

Praise for *The Judging Porch*

"Rachael Dubinsky's debut chapbook, *The Judging Porch*, is a meditation on finding hope and healing when the outside world is chaotic, and our relationships grow complicated. Using short, succinct poems, Dubinsky offers windows into our emotions, from confusion and grief to "persistent love" and "turbulent hope." She minds us that the homes we create are the spaces where we can be vulnerable, reclaim our authentic voices, and "Walk down/A lush path/Steeped in/Goodmemories/Never to be taken for granted."

—*Sara Letourneau, author of Wild Gardens*

"In *The Judging Porch*, Rachael Dubinsky explores what it feels like when reality shatters a valued perception. Her poems grapple with the process of reconciling these two realities, holding both the depths of grief and the joy of healing in their short and powerful lines. This chapbook gives voice to some of those innermost thoughts and intimate experiences that, while painful at the time, can be liberating when shared.

—*Dr. Kimberly Sterin, education researcher*

The Judging Porch

By Rachael Dubinsky

First published by Wicked Writers 2024

Copyright © 2024 by Rachael Dubinsky

All rights reserved. No part of this publication may be reproduced, stored or transmitted in any form or by any means, electronic, mechanical, photocopying, recording,   scanning, or otherwise without written permission from the publisher. It is illegal to copy this book, post it to a website, or distribute it by any other means without permission.

First edition
ISBN 979-8-9909993-0-5

Table of Contents

For my rocks — Mom, Lauren, Dan
And my pebbles — Parker, Riley, Maisie

Forward

There once was a porch in Medford, Massachusetts.

Now this was no ordinary outdoor structure, it was a magical porch, towering above the street, watching passersby.

Until one day in March 2020, when the world shutdown due to a global pandemic, and the once active street where this porch stood, retreated into quiet solitude, like the rest of the world.

Also at this time, a boy and a girl moved into a new apartment, hoping to chart new water in their young relationship. Little did they realize one of the most important spaces was outside the walls of their shared dwelling.

An open-air fortress - the porch was decorated with sparkly string lights, a rug and swivel chairs.

Many occasions were marked from the porch - walk-by Birthday parades, late-night dinners, festive Fall decorating parties. A safe space to celebrate, to reflect, to grieve.

Solace during the darkness.

A beacon of light guiding me to this place, right here, right now – my first poetry chapbook.

And thus, The Judging Porch was born.

If you know a narcissist — this one's for you.

No, *You're* Disrespectful.

You must earn
respect
to get
respect

Nothing is given.

Parent
Sibling
Cousin
Childhood best friend

Respect is an acknowledgement
of acceptance

A choice
We can revoke
At any moment

Everything is taken
When conditions apply.

A Prayer for Hope.

What's false about hope?

When it fails
It leaves you
Feeling helpless

What's false about hope?

It keeps you holding on
To something
That may no longer be there

What's false about hope?

In your desperate search
For answers
To circumstances
Beyond your control

You lose yourself.

What's true about hope?

It's tried
It's unrelenting

Annoyingly so.

What's true about hope?

It breathes life
Into our souls

Belief is ours to hold on to

Smoke and Mirrors.

Mirror mirror on the wall

Can we conceal
The depths of your lies
Hidden in the shadows
Of my truth

Mirror mirror on the wall

My purpose
Is to put on a good face
For no reason
Other than to keep the peace

Mirror mirror on the wall

My posture may be
Calm and collected
But there will always be
A voice screaming

This is not normal.

Monster.

Your existence sends
Pins and needles
Straight into my
Vulnerable brain

The "what ifs" and
Pervasive anger

Is destined to curse me
Forever

It didn't look "wrong"
From the outside

It was the secret manipulation
That strangled our relationship

The very thought
Of your oblivious existence
Haunts me to this very day

My only solace: I got to walk away.

A Mind of Your Own.

You are never
Too young
To form your own
Thoughts and opinions
Because that is what it means
To be human

Don't blend in
Stand out
Challenge a system
Not meant
For any woman

Loud or quiet.

Brain Games.

You don't have to accept
Your thoughts
At face value

In fact, our minds
Are meant to be transformed.

Trouble Trip.

Here we are
On an island of loneliness
With no place
For hard feelings

Wash away your fear
With a tide of turbulent hope
A wave of wanting
Carrying us to the future

As we walk down
A lush path
Steeped in
Good memories
Never to be taken for granted.

RIP, Dear Friend.

I may not remember
What made you laugh
Or what made you cry

I will remember
Your miles-wide smile
Your gentle nature
Your incredible fashion sense
Your unparalleled work ethic

You were a treasure
Shining a light
On all who knew you

Our planet is worse for having lost you

A journey
Cut short
Due to a healthcare system
That has unfairly
Taken you and so many others.

In memory of Arika Trim.

Silence is the Enemy.

I was loud
Until I was quiet

Losing myself
To thoughts
And feelings
I couldn't clear from my own head

I was strong
Until I was weak

Forgetting
My superpower

Resilience.

I was angry
Until I was sad

Hoping
To escape the pain

If I get swallowed whole
In my silence
I might not survive.

Silhouette.

Silence is a twisted sentence
For the broken hearted

I feel like a figment
Of past me

A fraction
Of my old self
Outlined in remorse

Quiet hearts
Make for even louder thoughts.

Puzzle Pieces.

How does it feel
When you put the pieces together
Only for them to break apart again

Over and over

We rebuild
And like clockwork
Plans and dreams collapse

A picture develops
Piece by piece

The process
Moving at a glacial pace

Patience tested
Patterns emerge
And blend together
Into a beautiful collage.

On Vulnerability.

The energy of the universe
Is waiting
For your spirit
To be unleashed

Exposed
Wounds of the past

Make way
For you
To achieve your wildest dreams
Of a healed future.

Hold Me.

I am trusting you
To heal my heart

A responsibility
Not to be taken lightly
And likely to be
Tested from time to time

I want your honesty
And soft touch
To hold me
As I rebuild

It seems too easy to love you

Maybe the challenge
Was invented
In my head
The whole time.

Privilege and Pain.

How lucky am I?

That I can dedicate time
To think about
The space I take up

A passing storm
No longer
A category five hurricane
Of emotions

I am grateful
For time well spent
Dedicated
To reflection and renewal

Mild temperatures on the rise
Put me
Back together again.

Inner Voices.

Quiet criticism
Creeps in
Like the spider on your ceiling
That's only bothersome
Once the creepy crawler
Makes its presence known

Let it settle
And unwind
The webs
Of regret

Spinning a new story
Where you have nothing to fear.

Let's Be Real.

It's all a facade

The posts
The interactions
The passive likes and comments

We have lost
The soul of community
In our quest
For quick dopamine hits

Putting ourselves on a pedestal
Shattered
In the face of judgment

Let's recommit
To our intentions
Of supporting
One another

Muffled.

"I can't hear you"
Becomes my anthem

Really?!
Because it sounds
Like I'm screaming in my head

How can I reclaim my voice?

To resuscitate
Communication
Between myself
And the outside world.

The Pain in Rain.

Water
Drips down my face
Into a pool of sorrow

Begging to be splashed
Around
Drenching me
In disappointment.

Smoke and Mirrors Pt. 2.

No one wants to be made a fool
No one deserves less than the truth
No one can take away your power or purpose

Going at the speed of light
Someone is bound to be left behind

Wondering

Why wasn't I enough?

Where did it all go wrong?

Home.

My home is wherever you are
And I belong
In the comfort of your gaze

We have an understanding

We are here,
Together,
In this moment
For a reason

This vision of our life
Slowly turning into reality
Will ebb and flow
With time and space

Our persistent love
Continuing to guide us home.

Acknowledgements

Books don't happen in a vacuum. I'm incredibly grateful
to those who helped me along the way.

Editor
Caitlin Conlon

Cover Design
Anze Ban Virant

Interior Formatting & Design
Robert Thibeault, Abdul Wasay

About the Author

Rachael Dubinsky is a poet, artist and founder of Wicked Writers, a consulting group focused on creating compelling written content for creative thought leaders and mission-based organizations. She has a weekly newsletter, #WickedWednesdays, focused on storytelling, lifting up marginalized voices and sharing local community resources in New England. Her writing has been featured in Toastmasters Magazine, Jewish Women's Archive and Scout Somerville. Rachael resides in Framingham, Mass. with her husband, Dan, and their dog, Parker.

The Judging Porch is her first poetry chapbook. A version of the poem, *A Prayer for Hope*, will appear in *Solitude, Community, Hope: An Anthology.*

Her work is available at **www.rachaeldubinsky.com**.

To learn more about Wicked Writers, visit www.wickedwriters.com and sign up for #WickedWednesdays at wickedwriters.substack.com.

www.ingramcontent.com/pod-product-compliance
Lightning Source LLC
Chambersburg PA
CBHW051337120626
46547CB00016B/2589